TWELVE TOPICS FOR ESL BEGINNERS

Teacher Guide

Glenda Reece
ESL Training Services
Raleigh, NC USA
www.eslts.com

ISBN-10 0-9842813-2-0
ISBN-13 978-0-9842813-2-9

CONTENTS

TEACHER PREFACE

New Student Information

When you start with a new student, it is important to obtain and keep a record of their name, address, phone number, and email address. Most ESL programs have a Personal Information Form of some sort to accomplish this. If you are teaching outside of an organized program, you will need to create a form for this purpose. Getting an accurate phone number and email address, and providing your own phone number and email address will allow communication if schedule changes are needed. An email address also allows you to remind students of the class and keep them coming.

Student Oral Proficiency Rating and Placement

Although not covered in this book, proper rating of the student's oral proficiency, and proper placement into a class of the correct level is very important; however, if a student feels that he/she has been placed in the wrong level, you need to respond by discussing the original decision, and , if necessary, moving that student into a different class.

Cultural Issues

One very important issue when working with ESL Beginners is that they are not stupid just because they do not know English. Do not treat adult students as children. Do not use materials with an adult if the materials were made for children. Do not talk down to them.

In many cultures, pride and honor are critical parts of an individual's life to a greater extent that with Americans. Also, the most important things in life for them may be their relationships with family and friends. In America, we tend to ask new acquaintances what they do, what is their job. In many cultures, work is not an issue; family, including ancestors, are the most important issues and form the basis for relationships.

Language Needs for ESL Beginners

The first of many things a new international needs to be able to communicate is the information included in their Personal Information Form, plus greetings: their name address, phone number and email address, and how we say "Hello, how are you today?" Beyond that, they must be able to speak about basic needs such as food and how to shop for it, dates and times, body parts, pain and medical information. They must learn how to respond to emergencies, contact various government offices such as the police, fire departments, hospitals, and their own embassy. This book is designed to provide you with material you can use to create lessons for your students in most of these areas.

Topics, Not Lessons

Each topic contains a selection of content and practice material. To create lessons, you must pick and choose material from different parts of a topic based on the specific needs of your students.

How to Create and Use Lessons

Although the book is designed to cover most of the areas mentioned in the previous paragraphs, it is not divided into lessons. As the teacher you must pick and choose from the material and create lessons based on the specific needs of your students.

Each topic contains enough material for several lessons. For example, most topics contain many vocabulary words, but a beginning student can only learn seven to twelve words in a given lesson; and those words must be repeated many, many times in the lesson, and then repeated many times again in review sessions in the following three or four lessons.

In a single lesson, select appropriate words from the Vocabulary section or other words from your own knowledge of the student's needs. Do not teach vocabulary as single words and their definition; instead, teach phrases that will be useful and that are related to the vocabulary word.

Expand the lesson to include one or two items found in the *Reading and Speaking Exercise* sections, or other verses or chants that you create. And with most students, you will want to include writing practice that fits in with the other content of the lesson.

Teacher and Student Books

The teacher book and the student book are the same except that the Preface and Teacher Notes are only in the Teacher version of the books. The student book does not contain a preface at all, and contains only Student Goals and a blank page for notes and practice writing. (these keep the page numbers the same in both books.)

In all lessons, the real keys are:

1. The student must do a lot of talking. Never lecture where you talk and the students just listen. Instead, get them involved in everything you do. Again, teach phrases or sound units and use the Rule of Five:

    1) *You say something* five times

    2) You have the *student say it with you* five times

    3) Have the *student say it without you* five times

    4) You listen and make corrections

    5) Have the *student say it five times more.*

2. Repeat the last two steps as many times as needed. Most phrases will require a student to repeat the phrase thirty to fifty times before it sounds like you. As a native speaker, you are the gold standard so you want your student to sound like you. Use the phrase, "Sound like me. I want you to sound like me."

3. Remember, it's not just pronunciation. It's also the rhythm of the language, the volume, the pitch, and the stamina to actually say the entire phrase all the way to the end and not let the ending get truncated or drop out. Americans speak louder than many cultures and with a lower pitch. Your students need to sound like Americans.

4. Remember:

    1) *Repetition—Use the rule of five*

    2) *Make the students do the talking*

    3) *Teach sound units and phrases instead of single words*

    4) *It's more than pronunciation: teach rhythm, volume, pitch, and stamina*

    5) *You are the gold standard—your students need to sound like you.*

TOPIC ONE TEACHER NOTES

Goals for the Student

- Be able to speak first and last names, address, and phone number in English.
- Spell name, street name, city, and state
- Write name and address
- Respond to basic greetings and introductions

Notes to the teacher

As mentioned in the Preface, the Personal Information Form and the placement interview are the core of this first topic. Here the students will have some exposure to the information individually.

Expect chaos for the first several class meetings. It takes a while to get everyone seated, information sheets filled out, name tags written, etc. Many of the students will be nervous and the teachers need an extra dose of patience and tolerance.

Vocabulary

Students don't need to understand every word that is spoken, but do need to learn key words as quickly as possible. Introduce the new vocabulary with body language, gestures, visuals and objects whenever possible. A few words of translation is OK, if necessary and available; otherwise, stick to the target language–English!

Suggestions

1. Write the nouns on cards. Have real objects like pencils, papers, books, chairs, perhaps a cell phone.
2. Put numbers on cards and mix them up. Have them read the numbers. Use any excuse you can think of to have students learn numbers 1-12. (Preparation for telling time.) Write the numbers on the board and mix them up.

3. Teach spelling. Have the students read the spelling off the cards. Book = b-o-o-k, etc.
4. Teach "This is a _______." and "It's a book" using the cards. Teach them What is this? And "What's this?" Have them chain drill the question and answer.
5. Remember: *this* you can touch, and *that* is too far away to touch.
6. Teach, *"I don't know." "I don't understand."* Use elaborate gestures for negatives.
7. Model the dialog with a role play and gestures.
8. If they already know the above:
   a. Say the names of the alphabet letters. Identify letters out of order. A, P, D, T, S, B instead of A, B, C, D, E, F, etc. Count the numbers to 10, then to 20, by 10's to 100., etc. Name the letters in a student's name, or all student's if the class is small.
   b. Spell several of the words, and have the students ask you questions.

Reading and Writing Exercises

1. Write the dialog and some of the vocabulary words on the board.
2. Read the words and point to them. Have the students repeat.
3. Write letters of the alphabet. Say them. If the class can follow, sing the children's alphabet song
4. *Small Talk,* by Carolyn Graham (About $26.00, Oxford University Press.), is an excellent resource for teaching beginner levels. In this manual I have written several chants to be used in the same way to teach speed and rhythm of American English.

TOPIC ONE:
Introductions, Greetings, Alphabet, Numbers

VOCABULARY

Verbs	Nouns		
1. Is, are	1. Name	7. Hello	13. Chair
2. Has, have	2. Name tag	8. Pencil	14. Book
3. Work	3. Restroom	9. Paper	15. Table
4. Need	4. Bathroom	10. Number	
5. Write	5. Toilet	11. Phone	
6. Spell	6. Address	12. Cell phone	

Question words	Demonstratives
1. who, what	1. this, that

READING AND SPEAKING EXERCISE

Greetings, Names, Addresses, Questions

1. Hello. How are you?
   Fine, thanks. How are you?
   Fine, thanks.

2. My name is _______.
   What is your name?
   Who is he? (or she)
   He is _______.

3. This is a _______.
   What is this?
   I don't know.

4. My address is _______.
   What is your address?
   I don't understand.

Hi! How Are You?
from *Small Talk*
by Carolyn Graham

Hi! How are you?
Fine. How are you?

Hi! How are you?
Fine. How are you?

Hi! How are you?

Hi! How are you?

Hi! How are you?
Fine. How are you?

Where Do You Live?
by Glenda Reece

Where do you live?
Where do you live?

I live on Main Street.
I live on Main Street.

Where do you live?
Where do you live?

I live on Main Street.
I live on Main Street.

Where do you live?
Where do you live?

I live on _____ Street.

The ABC Song

A-B-C-D-E-F-G
H-I-J-K, L-M-N-O-P
Q-R-S, T-U-V
W-X, Y and Z.
Now I know my ABC's
Next time won't you sing with me

COMPETENCY

- I can write my name in English.
- I can spell my name in English.
- I can give all the parts of my address: street number, street name, town, state and zip
- I can say "hi", "hello" and "good-bye". ("Hi" is the most used greeting.)
- I can say, "I don't know" and "I don't understand."

WRITING EXERCISE

Use the worksheet below to practice the following writing and speaking exercises.

Write your name in English.

Write the letters B, O, and K (uppercase and lowercase)

Write the word: BOOK (uppercase and lowercase).

Learn the name and sound of the letters B, O, and K.

Write the numbers 1, 2, 3, 4, and 5 as words and as numbers (one 1, two 2, three 3, four 4, five 5).

Write your name, in English, in each of the spaces below

Write the letter *B* (uppercase) and *b* (lowercase) in all of the spaces below.

B b				

Write the letters *O* (uppercase) and *o* (lowercase) in all of the spaces below.

O o				

Write the letters *K* (uppercase) and *k* (lowercase) in all of the spaces below.

K k				

Write the words: *BOOK* (uppercase) and *book* (lowercase) in all of the spaces below.

BOOK book				

Give the name of the letter, and speak the *sound* of the letter.

1. The name of the letter is "B"; and the sound of the letter is (speak the *sound, not the name.* for example, speak the beginning *sound* of the word *Book.*). (repeat at least ten times)
2. The name of the letter is "O"; and the sound of the letter is (speak the *sound, not the name.* for example, speak the beginning *sound* of the word *Only.*). (repeat at least ten times)
3. The name of the letter is "K"; and the sound of the letter is (speak the *sound, not the name.* for example, speak the beginning *sound* of the word *Kite.*). (repeat at least ten times)

Write the name and number for *1, 2, 3, 4, 5* in all of the spaces below.

ONE 1				
ONE 1				
TWO 2				
TWO 2				
THREE 3				
THREE 3				
FOUR 4				
FOUR 4				
FIVE 5				
FIVE 5				

TOPIC TWO TEACHER NOTES

Goals for the Student

- Answer job related questions.
- Know social security number and date of birth.
- Write name, social security number, and date of birth.
- Respond to basic greetings and introductions.
- Begin learning vocabulary for parts of the body and health information.
- Say the numbers 1-10.

Notes to the teacher

The second topic continues teaching the information found on forms such as registration and job applications.

Continue to expect chaos for the first several class meetings. Students may begin to bring their friends. Often, welcoming is done in the reception area with great confusion. Smile and hang in there.

Suggestions

1. Write the nouns on cards. Have an application, a social security card, and a driver's license to show the students.
2. Use an outline drawing of the body. Teach only the major words first. Rule of thumb: 5 body part words at a time and review.
3. Choose several words to spell. Do a chain drill with This word is_______. Please spell it.
4. Teach who is for people, what is for objects, and where is for place.
5. Review, I don't know. I don't understand. Teach: It's not a _______.
6. Act out point, shake, and scratch. Have entire class point at body parts, and objects they know.

7. Write the model sentence on the board. Use a calendar and teach: Today is <*use the current month, day, and year*> It is <*use the current day of the week*>.
8. If they already know the above:
   a. Talk about applications and social security numbers.
   b. Add several words to parts of the body. (Hair, mouth, nose, ear, lips, etc.)

Reading and Writing Exercises

1. Write the dialog and some of the vocabulary words on the board.
2. Read the words and point to them.
3. Have the students repeat.
4. Review the alphabet song.
5. Draw the outline of a body. Have students write the body parts.

Competency

- I can write my birth date.
- I can say three parts of the body.
- I can write my Social Security number.
- I can ask What's your name? And give my name.
- I can say, "It's not a ____.
- I can copy several words in English.

Materials You Will Need

- Use Board and Markers to write on. Otherwise, a flip chart or some substitute.
- Drawing of body to label parts of body
- Pictures of Social Security card, driver's license, etc.
- Have any handouts you chose copied and ready for your class.
- Index cards with drills on them.

TOPIC TWO:
Work

(Also includes a review of Topic One)

VOCABULARY

Verbs	Nouns	
1. Live	1. Date of birth	7. Head
2. Point	2. Social Security number	8. Arms
3. Shake	3. Driver's license number	9. Legs
4. Scratch	4. Age	10. Body, trunk
5. Drive	5. Month	11. Job
6. Go, went	6. Day	12. (Your city)

Question words	Demonstratives
1. Who	1. This
2. What	2. That
3. Where	3. These
4. When	4. Those

READING AND SPEAKING EXERCISE

Names, Addresses, Greetings, Questions

1. Hello. How are you?
   Fine, thanks. How are you?
   Fine, thanks.

2. My name is ________.
   What is your name?
   Who is he? (or she)
   He is ________.

3. This is a ________.
   What is this?
   I don't know.

4. My address is ________.
   What is your address?
   I don't understand.

Sentences (insert different words in the blank spaces)

1. I have a _______. (book, pencil, etc.)
2. Do you have a _______? Please, give me a _______.
   Yes, I have a _______.
3. No, I don't have a _______.
4. Where do you live?
5. I live in _______. Do you live in _______?
6. Did you work today?
7. Where did you work today?
8. Did you drive today?
9. Where did you drive today?
10. Point to your _______. (head, etc.)
11. Shake your _______.
12. Scratch your _______.
13. Move to the right (left.)
14. Today is _____, (the date). It is a _______. (day of the week)

Alphabet

What is the *name* of the following letters?

M T P G D A O

What *sound* does each letter make?

REVIEW

The ABC Song

A-B-C-D-E-F-G H-I-J-K, L-M-N-O-P
Q-R-S, T-U-V W-X, Y and Z.
Now I know my ABC's, Next time won't you sing with me

Action Chant - Reece

Do this with me:
Shake your head
Shake your arm.
Shake your foot.

Do this with me:
Point your head.
Point your arm.
Point your foot.

Do you understand?
Do you understand?

I don't understand.
I don't understand.

Do this with me:
Shake your head.
Shake your arm.
Shake your foot.

Do this with me:
Move to the right
Move to the left.
Point your head.
Shake your head.

Do you understand?

Now, I understand.
Now, I understand.

Do You Work?

Do you work?
No, I need a job.
Do you know of one?

Do you work?
No I need a job.
If you hear of one,
Will you tell me, please?

Do you have a job?
Yes, I do. I work on a farm.
I work for Mr. Jones.

I need a job.
If he has a job,
Let me know, OK?

Sure. I'll tell Mr. Jones.
Sure. I'll tell him.

Good-bye, Good-bye

Good-bye, good-bye.
See you tomorrow.
Bye-bye.

Good-bye,
see you tomorrow.

Good-bye,
see you tomorrow.

Bye-bye.
See you tomorrow.

So long,
see you tomorrow.

So long,
see you tomorrow.

Bye-bye.

What's This?

What's this?

I don't know.
I don't know.

It's a pencil.

Oh. It's a pencil.
Oh. It's a pencil.

What's this?

I don't know.
I'm not sure.

It's a book.

Oh. It's a book.
Oh. It's a book.

What's this?

I don't know.
I don't know.
I'm not sure.

Try to remember.

It's a chair.

Who Stole the Cookie?

(1st Person says:)
Who stole the cookie
from the cookie jar?

<name of 2nd person>
stole the cookie
from the cookie jar.

(2nd Person Says:)
Not me!

(1st Person says:)
Then who?

(2nd Person Says:)
<name of 3rd person>
stole the cookie
from the cookie jar.

(3rd Person Says:)
Not me!

(2nd Person says:)
Then who?

(3rd Person Says:)
<name of 4th person>
stole the cookie
from the cookie jar.

(continue around the room until everyone has participated.)

WRITING EXERCISE

Write your name in English.

Write the letters, W, R, L, I, V, E, and the words Work, Live, What.

Write the question, What is that?

Write the numbers 6, 7, 8, 9 and 10 as words and as numbers (six 6, seven 7, eight 8, nine 9, ten 10).

Learn the name and sound of the letters A, L, I, V, D, and P.

Write your name, in English, in all of the spaces below

Write the letters *W* (uppercase) and *w* (lowercase) in all of the spaces below.

W w				

Write the letters *R* (uppercase) and *r* (lowercase) in all of the spaces below.

R r				

Write the letters *L* (uppercase) and *l* (lowercase) in all of the spaces below.

L l				

Write the letters *I* (uppercase) and *i* (lowercase) in all of the spaces below.

I i				

Write the letters *V* (uppercase) and *v* (lowercase) in all of the spaces below.

V v				

Write the letters *E* (uppercase) and *e* (lowercase) in all of the spaces below.

E e				

Write the words: *WORK* (uppercase) and *work* (lowercase) in all of the spaces below.

WORK work				

Write the words: *LIVE* (uppercase) and *live* (lowercase) in all of the spaces below.

LIVE live				

Write the words: *WHAT* (uppercase) and *what* (lowercase) in all of the spaces below.

WHAT what				

Write the sentence, *What is this?,* in all of the spaces below.

What is this?	

Write the name and number for *6, 7, 8, 9, 10* in the spaces below.

SIX 6				
SIX 6				
SEVEN 7				
SEVEN 7				
EIGHT 8				
EIGHT 8				
NINE 9				
NINE 9				
TEN 10				
TEN 10				

Give the name of the letter, and speak the *sound* of the letter.

1. The name of the letter is "A"; and the sound of the letter is (speak the *sound, not the name.* for example, speak the beginning *sound* of the word *Apple.* (repeat at least ten times)
2. The name of the letter is "L"; and the sound of the letter is (speak the *sound, not the name.* for example, speak the beginning *sound* of the word *Live.* (repeat at least ten times)
3. The name of the letter is "V"; and the sound of the letter is (speak the *sound, not the name.* for example, speak the beginning *sound* of the word *Very.* (repeat at least ten times)
4. The name of the letter is "D"; and the sound of the letter is (speak the *sound, not the name.* for example, speak the beginning *sound* of the word *Dog.* (repeat at least ten times)
5. The name of the letter is "P"; and the sound of the letter is (speak the *sound, not the name.* for example, speak the beginning *sound* of the word *Pet.* (repeat at least ten times)

TOPIC THREE TEACHER NOTES

Goals for the Student

- Name and identify major parts of the body
- Give the date
- Spell and write name and address information
- Repeat and begin to memorize days of the week.
- Begin use of pronouns
- Learn the verb to be.
- Say numbers 1-12 and 0. Repeat page numbers, any excuse to say a number

Notes to the teacher

The third topic should review the information found on forms such as registration and job applications. Also begin health information, body names, and pronouns.

Suggestions

1. Use a calendar. Read the days of the week. Give the students cards labeled with the names of the days, and have them line up the cards in the correct order. Let them work it out.
2. Write the nouns on cards. Have pictures or touch the window, door, etc.
3. Use an outline drawing of the body. Teach only a few words at a time.
4. Play Simon says to teach body parts. Have a student lead it as soon as possible. Laugh a lot.
5. Memorize the verb to be. Drill it many times using the names of the students in the room. See if students can do it themselves. Give a prize, if possible, something like a stick of gum. Use this drill to teach the pronouns, I, you, he, she, it, we, you, they.

6. Teach where and the prepositions on and in. Use the nouns they know. Put a pencil on a book. Teach on. Put the pencil in the book. Teach in. Chain drill this so all students say: Where is the pencil. It is on (in) the book.
7. Review *point, shake, and scratch.* Teach *touch.* Act out *It hurts.* Teach *My ________hurts. My leg hurts,* etc. (Use a band aid.)
8. Have entire class point at body parts, and objects they know.
9. Act out (TPR) open and close. Use doors, windows, books, etc. or anything that opens and closes. Teach the commands: Open the door. Close the door. Open your book. Close your book.
10. Write the model sentences on the board. Use a calendar and teach *Today is <use the current month, day, and year>. It is <use the current day of the week>. My head doesn't hurt. Please open the door. I like English Class. My teacher is ________.*
11. If they already know the above:
    a. Put all the verbs learned so far into statements, questions, and negatives.
    b. Practice using the prepositions in and on. Make positive and negative statements using the prepositions. Is the book on the table? No, it isn't.

Reading and Writing Exercises

1. Draw the outline of a body. Have students write the body parts.
2. Have the students copy the verb to be.
3. Have the students write a verb with the pronouns. Ex: *I touch,* etc.

Materials You Will Need

- Markers to write with and board to write on. Otherwise, a flip chart or some substitute.
- Calendar, picture for parts of the body.
- Box, or can or something to demonstrate prepositions, in, on.
- Have any handouts you chose copied and ready for your class.
- Nouns written on cards, pictures or actual objects, window, door, etc.

TOPIC THREE:
Parts of the Body, Days of the Week

VOCABULARY

Verb *To Be*	Examples
1. I am .... We are	I am O.K. We are happy.
2. You are .... You are	You are O.K. You are happy.
3. He is .... They are	He is O.K. They are happy.
4. She is .... They are	She is O.K. They are happy.

Verbs	Nouns	
1. Touch	1. Hand	6. Mouth
2. Hurt, hurts	2. Foot	7. Window
3. Come	3. Knee	8. Door
4. Open	4. Elbow	9. Floor
5. Close	5. Eye	10. Light

Question Words	Examples
1. Who	Who hurts? Does anyone hurt
2. What	What were you doing? I was running.
3. When	When did it happen? Five minutes ago
4. Where	Where do you hurt? My knee hurts.
5. Why	Why does it hurt? I fell on a rock.

Prepositions

1. On
2. In

Days of the Week

Sunday, Monday, Tuesday, Wednesday, Thursday, Friday, Saturday

Weekend, weekday

READING AND SPEAKING EXERCISE

Statements and Questions

1. I have a _______.
   Do you have a _______?
   Yes, I have a _______.
   (or No, I don't)

2. What did you touch?
   I touched my ._______.

3. What day is today?
   Today is _____.
   Is it *Wednesday*.
   No, it isn't. It's *Tuesday*.
   Yes, it is.

4. Open the door.
   Open the book.
   Close the door.
   Close the book

5. Touch your head.
   Touch your hand.
   Touch your arm.

6. I live in _______.
   Do you live in _______?
   Where do you live?

7. Point to your _______.
   Shake your _______.
   Scratch your _______.

8. I am _______ *name.*
   You are _______ *name.*
   He is_______ *name.*
   She is _______ *name.*
   etc.

9. I am O.K.
   I am happy.
   Are you O.K?
   Are you happy?

10. Where is the book?
    It is on the table.
    Where is the pencil?
    It is on the book.
    (or it is in the book.)

JAZZ CHANTS

Who, What Were, When, Why *from* Small Talk *by Carolyn Graham*

Who?, What?, When?
Where?, Why?, Why?

Who?, What?, When?
Where?, Why?, Why?

Who did it?
What did he do?

Where did he do it?
Why?

Who did it?
What did he do?

Where did he do it?
Why?

Who did it?
What did he do?

Where did he do it?
Why?

Open the Door, Please *by Glenda Reece*

Hey, Jose,
Open the door.
Open the door, please.

What did you say?
What did you say?
I didn't hear you.

I didn't hear you.
Say it again.
Say it again.

Open the door.
Open the door, please.

What did you say?
What did you say?
I didn't hear you.

I didn't hear you.
Say it again.
Say it again.

I said, open the door.

Oh. Open the door.
OK.

Oh. Open the door.
OK.

Hey, Jorge,
Close the door.
Close the door, please.

What did you say?
What did you say?
I didn't hear you.

I didn't hear you.
Say it again.
Say it again.

Close the door.
Close the door, please.

COMPETENCY

- I can name several parts of the body.
- I can correctly use open and close.
- I know the words: door, window, floor.
- I know the name of the first day of the week. (Sunday).
- I can make a question.

WRITING EXERCISE

Write a question.

Write the words: Touch, Arm, Head, Elbow, Point.

Write the numbers: eleven 11, twelve 12, and zero, 0 as words and as numbers.

Learn the name and sound of the letters P, Y, Z, and B

Write the question: *Hi, how are you?*, in all of the spaces below.

Hi, how are you?	

Write the word: *touch* in all of the spaces below.

touch				

Write the word: *arm* in all of the spaces below.

arm				

Write the word: *head* in all of the spaces below.

head				

Write the word: *elbow* in all of the spaces below.

elbow				

Write the word: *point* in all of the spaces below.

point				

Write: *I live on <u>(your street)</u>*, in all of the spaces below.

I live on ______________________ street.

Write the name and number for *11,12,* and *0* below.

ELEVEN 11			
ELEVEN 11			
TWELVE 12			
TWELVE 12			
ZERO 0			
ZERO 0			

Write parts of the body that you know.

1. ______________
2. ______________
3. ______________
4. ______________
5. ______________
6. ______________
7. ______________
8. ______________

TOPIC FOUR TEACHER NOTES

Goals for the Student

- Say, My (arm, leg, etc.) hurts. I don't feel good. I'm sick.
- Review date on a calendar
- Know two ways to say the time
- Begin use of possessive pronouns
- Form a question, make a statement, and form a negative verb.
- Use the verb do, did.

Notes to the teacher

The fourth topic reviews names and addresses. Also continue body names and body names; and begin health complaints and how to take medicine.

Suggestions

1. Draw a circle for a clock. As students say 1 – 12, write in the numbers. Teach the hours and have them repeat. Point and ask, *What time is it?*
2. Use an outline drawing of the body. Review names of the body areas.
3. Drill verbs like fixed, and broken.
4. Memorize the verb *to do*. Drill it and also review the verb *to be* many times using the names of the students in the room.
5. Teach *where* and *over* and *under*. Review *on* and *in*. Use the nouns they know.
6. Review *It hurts*. Review My ________hurts. My leg hurts., etc. Have entire class point at body parts, and objects they know. (Sometimes I use a Band-Aid and move it around for them to understand).
7. If they already know the above:
   a. Put all the verbs learned so far into statements, questions, and negatives.

Reading and Writing Exercises

1. Write model sentence on the board. Use a calendar and teach: *Today is <use the current month, day, and year>. It is <use the current day of the week>. What time is it? I don't have a watch. My friend has a digital watch. I use my cell phone. My watch is broken. I need it fixed.*
2. Have the students copy the verb to do. Drill it. Statement, question, negative.
3. After having students complete the entire alphabet (uppercase and lowercase) in the book, have them repeat the process on a blank sheet od paper without the example letters that are in the exercise printed in the book.

Materials You Will Need

- Clock (cardboard or drawing) that you can turn hands on.
- Calendar
- A broken object, such as a cup, or watch, etc.
- Have any handouts you chose copied and ready for your class.
- Band-Aids to teach *It hurts.*

TOPIC FOUR:
Parts of the Body; Pain, and Complaints

VOCABULARY

Verb *To Do*	Examples
1. I do, We do	I do good work. We do good work.
2. You do, You do	You do good work. You do good work.
3. He does, They do	He does good work. They do good work.
4. She does, They do	She does good work. They do good work.
5. It does, They do	It does good work. They do good work.

Verbs	Nouns	
1. Break	1. Time	6. Clock
2. Broken	2. O'clock	7. Watch
3. Fix, fixed	3. Hour	8. Number
4. Need	4. Minute	9. Cup
5. Close	5. Second	

Question Words	Demonstratives	Prepositions
1. Who	1. This	1. On
2. What	2. That	2. In
3. Where	3.These	3. Over
4. When	4. Those	4. Under

READING AND SPEAKING EXERCISE

1. What time is it?
   It's _______two o'clock.
   It's _______two fifteen.
2. My watch is broken.
   Can you fix it?

3 My watch is fixed.
Thank you.

4 Point to your _______.

5. Shake your _______.

6. Scratch your _______.

Statement	Question	Answer
I need my book.	Do I need my book	Yes, you do.
He needs his book.	Does he need his book?	Yes, he does.
She needs her book.	Does she need her book?	Yes, she does.
We need our books.	Do we need our books?	Yes, we do.
You need your book.	Do you need your book?	Yes, you do.
They need their books.	Do they need their books?	Yes, they do.
My watch is broken.	Can you fix my watch?	Yes, I can.

Health

My ________ hurts.

I don't feel good.

I'm sick.

What time is it?

What time is it?
What time is it?

I don't know.
My watch is broken.

What time is it?
What time is it?

I don't know.
Ask Tom.

What time is it?
What time is it?

Tom, Tom!
What time is it?

What time is it?
What time is it?

It's one o'clock.

What day is it?

What day is it?
What day is it?

Is it Sunday?
Is it Monday?

What day is it?
What day is it?

Is it Tuesday?
Is it Wednesday?

What day is it?
What day is it?

Is it Thursday?
Is it Friday?

What day is it?
What day is it?

It's Saturday!

Question	Statement	Negative
What's this?	This is a book	This is not a book. It is a pen.
What is ____?	This is a _____.	This is not a ____. It is a _____.

Have a student hold up a Pen, Book, Watch, or other object and ask another What 's this? *Stand up and walk around the room. and touch the door, a chair and other objects, and again say,* What's this? *(It's a chair, door, floor, window, etc.)*

COMPETENCY

- I can count from 1-12 in English, and I know the number 0.
- I can tell on-the-hour time.
- I know the words, *fixed* and *broken*.
- I know the days of the week.

WRITING EXERCISE

Write: *This isn't a book. This is not a book.* in all of the spaces below.

This isn't a book. This is not a book.

Write the words: *Chair, Table, Broken, and Happy* in the spaces provided.

Chair				
Table				
Broken				
Happy				

Write: *This isn't broken. This is not broken.* in the spaces.

This isn't broken. This is not broken.

Write: your street address in all of the spaces below

Write the uppercase alphabet: *A* through *Z* (one letter in each space) next to the letter that is already there.

ABCDEFGHIJKLMNOPQRSTUVWXYZ				A	B
C	D	E	F	G	H
I	J	K	L	M	N
O	P	Q	R	S	T
U	V	W	X	Y	Z

Write the lowercase alphabet: *a* through *z* (one letter in each space) next to the letter that is already there.

abcdefghijklmnopqrstuvwxyz				a	b
c	d	e	f	g	h
i	j	k	l	m	n
o	p	q	r	s	t
u	v	w	x	y	z

Write: *What day is it?* in all of the spaces below.

What day is it?

Write: *Today is (Sunday, Monday, Tuesday, Wednesday, Thursday, Friday, Saturday)* in the spaces below.

(Example: Wednesday) **Today is Wednesday**
(Sunday)
(Monday)
(Tuesday)
(Wednesday)
(Thursday)
(Friday)
(Saturday)

TOPIC FIVE TEACHER NOTES

Goals for the Student

- Name, in English, family members.
- Say, *He's my brother. His name is____. She's my____. her name is____.*
- Review on hour time. Add quarter before, quarter past time.
- Know colors
- Use the verb have, has, had.
- Know today, yesterday, tomorrow with days of the week.
- Ask How many ___ do you have?

Notes to the teacher

The fifth topic should review broken, fixed and some time questions. Combine as much as possible from the previous four topics.

Suggestions

1. Draw a circle on the board for a clock. Review 1 o'clock, etc. and have them repeat. Ask What time is it? Teach *quarter past, quarter till and fifteen past and fifteen till.*
2. Use an outline drawing of the body. Review names of the body areas.
3. Drill verbs like *fixed*, and *broken.*
4. Memorize the verb *to have*. Drill it many times using the family words. Have the students in the room tell who has a son, daughter, sister, etc.
5. Demonstrate *Give it to me* with a student.
6. Teach colors. Be sure to have objects with colors you plan to teach. Teach light and dark colors. Use eyes. He has blue eyes. He has light blue eyes.
7. Teach possessives. *My hair is black. My book is red. Your hair is___.*
8. Teach answers. *Yes, it is. No, it isn't.*
9. Practice vocabulary using pictures and helps. Have students ask each other questions. After each student has answered questions about his family, play a guessing game. *Which person has two children? Which person is not married. Which student has a boy? a girl? has black hair? Is tall? Is short?* Ask them the opposites: What's the opposite of *tall?* of *boy?* of *father?*, etc.

10. Please remember to gear the lessons to the ability of your group. Some will only be able to cover a small part of a lesson. It's better for them to learn a little rather than be overwhelmed by too much. Ask them for feedback. Did they understand? Was it too hard? Too easy? One technique is to draw a bullseye target and have them mark the place the lesson hit them. In the middle? Towards the outside or outside altogether?
11. If they already know the above:
    a. Work on the verb *to have* in past, present, and future tense. Teach *yesterday, today,* and *tomorrow.*

Reading and Writing Exercises

1. Write model sentence on the board. Use a clock: It's four fifteen. It is time for class to end. My mother is waiting for me. See you next week.
2. Have the students copy the verb to have. Drill it. Statement, question, and negative.

Competency

- I recognize and say three colors.
- I can tell "quarter past" time.
- I know the words for my family members.
- I know 3 opposites. light, dark, etc.
- I know the possessive pronouns, my book, etc.
- I know Yes, it is. & No it isn't.

Materials You Will Need

- Colored cloth or paper to teach the primary colors.
- Family pictures. Other pictures of people who could be aunts, uncles, etc.
- Objects they know, window, pencil, etc. to put colors on.
- Same old clock to learn time. And a calendar to review.
- Drill cards to teach statement, question, and negative.
- Stick of gum or candy for a treat.
- Ask them to bring a picture of their family. You might do the same. Then the family words can be more meaningful.

TOPIC FIVE:
Family, Colors

VOCABULARY

Verb *To have*	Examples
1. I have, We have	I have a book. We have a book.
2. You have, you have	You have a book, You have a book.
3. He or she has, they have	She has a book. They have a book.

Prepositions	Examples
1. with	I will go with you

Opposites

1. Older than, Younger than
2. Taller than, Shorter than
3. Old, Young
4. Tall, Short
5. Light, Dark

Nouns

1. Mother	6. Daughter	11. Blue
2. Father, dad	7. Aunt	12. Brown
3. Sister	8. Uncle	13. Black
4. Brother	9. Red.	14. Red
5. Son	10. Family	15. Yellow

Question words	Examples
1. Who	Who was with you?
2. What	What were you doing?
3. Where	Where did you go?

READING AND SPEAKING EXERCISE

What time is it?

What time is it?
It's a quarter past (two) .
It's a quarter till (five).
It's two o'clock.

My window is broken.
My window is broken.
Can you fix it?
Yes, I can.
No I can't.

My ____ is taller than I am.
My ____ is older than I am.
My ____ is lighter than I am.
(Son, mother, sister, etc.)

Whose child is this?

He's crying. He's crying.

Whose child is crying?
He's my younger brother.
He's my younger brother.
He's our child.

Whose child is this?

She's been so good.

She's been so good.

Whose child is this?
She's my sister's little girl.
She's my sister's little girl.
She's older than my child.
She's older than my child.

I have my mother with me

I have my mother with me.
He has his mother with ____
She has her father.
We have our sister.
You have your son.
They have their children.

How many children do you have?
I have ______ children.
I have ______ child.

What colors are your ________?
What color is your _______?
What color is his _______?
(pants, shirts, hair, etc.)

What color is it?

I have a pencil.
What color is it?
What color is it?

It's yellow.
It's a yellow pencil.

I have a jacket.
What color is it?
It's blue.
It's a blue jacket.

What color is this?
Is this yellow?
No. It's not yellow. It's blue.
No. It's not yellow. It's blue.

COMPETENCY

- I recognize and say three colors.
- I can tell "quarter past" time.
- I know the words for my family members.
- I know 3 opposites. *light, dark, etc.*
- I know the possessive pronouns, *my book*, etc.
- I know *Yes, it is.* & *No it isn't.*

WRITING EXERCISE

Write the Sentences: *Who is that? That is my sister.* in the spaces below

Who is that? That is my sister.

Write the words: *Brother, Sister, Father, Mother* in the spaces below.

Brother				
Sister				
Father				
Mother				

Write the Sentence: *What do you need?* in the spaces below

What do you need?

Write 5 sentences telling things that you need as shown in the example below.

Example: I need a pencil
1.
2.
3.
4.
5.

Write the words: *Shake, Touch, Young and Old* in the spaces.

Shake				
Touch				
Young				
Old				

Write the Sentence: *What can I do to help?* in the spaces below

What can I do to help?

Write the Sentences: *What do you have? I have a ______.* (book, pen, etc.) in the spaces below

What do you have? I have a pencil.

TOPIC SIX TEACHER NOTES

Goals for the Student

- Identify items of clothing in English.
- Identify some colors
- Say, *His shirt is blue.* And complete drills of other words with *color,* and *possessives*
- Tell time. by fives. Its five after one. It's five 'till one.
- Use *yesterday, today, tomorrow.*

Notes to the teacher

Review *broken, fixed* and some *time.* Combine as much as possible from the previous four topics.

Suggestions

1. Try to find a box of clothes or some pictures to illustrate the new vocabulary. Have the students identify the clothing after you've taught the new words. Let students pick out one item or picture they like, and one they don't like.
2. Total Physical Response (TPR): *Give me the shoes, Pass me the shirt.* Play a game: *Pass the ___.* Have students ask the question, *Will you give me a shirt, pants,* etc.
3. Drill *verbs* like *wear, pass,* etc. These verbs are easy to act out.
4. Have student say: *My daughter likes red blouses. My son likes blue jeans.,* etc.
5. Demonstrate *in front of, behind.* Play a *line* game. Line up students. Have them tell who is in front and who is behind by saying things like *The red blouse is in front of the blue shirt. The white shirt is behind the yellow shirt,* etc.
6. Review *colors* with the clothing. Review *possessive. My red shirt,* etc.
7. If they already know the above:
    a. Ask what they wore yesterday and today.

Reading and Writing Exercises

1. Write model sentences on the board. My mother likes dresses. She doesn't wear pants. She doesn't like pants. She wants me to wear dresses. My sister likes her yellow dress. Which dress do you like? How much does it cost?
2. Drill all the new verbs. Statement, question, negative.

Materials You Will Need

- Box of old clothes or pictures of clothing.
- Color items to review colors.
- Simon says: Touch your shirt, jeans, belt, etc.
- Have any handouts you chose copied and ready for your class.
- Something with a zipper and buttons.

Pronunciation tip

In the chant: *Why Don't You Wear It,* the *don't you* actually sounds like *don'tchew.* In conversational English, when the verb ends in a *T* sound, and the next word is *you* or *your*, link the /t/ with *you*, and it sounds like *chew.* /ch/

TOPIC SIX:
Clothing

VOCABULARY

Verbs	Example
1. To Like	I like white shirts.
2. To Need,	I need a new pair of pants.
3. To put on	I put on my coat when it is cold.
4. To take off	I take off my coat when it is warm.
5. To wear	I wear a suit on Sunday.
6. To fit	My hat is too big; it doesn't fit my head.

Review: Touch, point, I go today, I went yesterday

Prepositions	Questions
1. In front of	1. How much does it cost?
2. Behind	2. How much is it?

Opposites

1. Tight , Loose	4. Clean, Dirty
2. Too big, Too little	5. Early, Late
3. Pretty, Ugly	6. Young, Old

Nouns

1. Jeans

2. Shirt

3. Jacket

4. Shoes

5. Sandals

6. Dress

7. Blouse

8. Underwear

9. Umbrella

10. Belt

11. Socks

12. Pants, Slacks

13. Coat

14. Zipper

15. Buttons

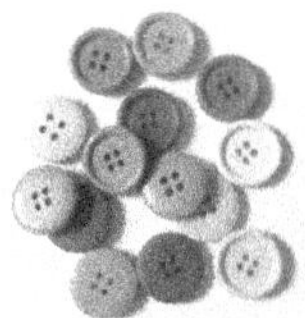

READING AND SPEAKING EXERCISE

I Need My Jacket

I need my jacket today.
Do I need my jacket?
No, it's too hot for a jacket.

I need a button.
What color do you need?

My zipper is broken.
My zipper is fixed
Can you fix it?

What color are your ____. (socks)
What color is your ____.
What color is his ____.

Where's my shirt?
I need my shirt.
I don't know.
Ask mom.

Where's my shoes?
Mom, where's my pretty shoes?
I don't know.
Ask Tom.

Tom, where's my yellow blouse?
Where's the clean clothes?
On the table.
Look on the table.

Thanks. Pass me my jacket.
Pass me my shoes.
Take off my shirt.
Take off my belt.
Your clothes are dirty.
My clothes are clean.

Why Don't You Wear It

My sister's jacket is ___.
I don't like red.
I don't like my pants.

Take off your jacket.
Put on your socks.

My ___ is too big.
My ___ is too little.
My shoes are tight.
His shoes are loose.

Are your shoes clean?
No, they're dirty.
Your shoes are pretty.
I think they are ugly.

Why don't you wear your new jacket?
Why don't you wear your new pants?
The jacket's too tight.
The pants are too loose.
I need clothes that fit.

Why don't you wear your new shoes?
Why don't you wear your new socks?
The shoes are too tight.
The socks are too big.

Why don't you wear the blue jeans?
The zipper is broken.
The button is gone.
Can you fix it?

Why don't you wear my old shirt?
The shirt is dirty.
I need clothes that are clean.

COMPETENCY

- I recognize clothing names of 4 or more items.
- I can tell five till and five after time.
- I know like, need, and wear.

WRITING EXERCISE

Write: *I like the red jacket. Do you like it?* in all of the spaces below.

I like the red jacket. Do you like it?

Write the words: *Jacket, Sandals, Shirt, and Dress* in the spaces provided.

Jacket				
Sandals				
Shirt				
Dress				

Write the sentence, *How much does it cost?,* in all of the spaces below.

How much does it cost?

Write *some things you need* in the spaces below

Socks	

Write the words: *Belt, Shoes, Zipper, Button and Umbrella* in the spaces provided.

Belt				
Shoes				
Zipper				
Button				
Umbrella				

Write the question: *How can I help you?*, in all of the spaces below.

How can I help you?

Write the sentences: *This doesn't fit right. I need another one.* in all of the spaces below.

This doesn't fit right. I need another one.

TOPIC SEVEN TEACHER NOTES

Goals for the Student

- Identify areas of the body in English.
- Say, *I feel sick, It's an emergency. Dial 911.*
- Know common physical complains, headache, sore throat, rash, fever, cramps.
- Use *yesterday, today, tomorrow.*

Notes to the teacher

The seventh topic should review parts of the body and verbs used in medical situations. Review as much as possible from the previous topics.

This topic can take weeks to teach, for it can cover many items. Students may open up and share needs. Those are true teaching moments.

Suggestions

1. Bring several items from your home medicine cabinet. Bring salve for a rash, aspirin, cough drops and something for heartburn or diarrhea. Often, just the empty box or carton is all you need. Show the items & demonstrate them.
2. TPR or act out the nouns and verbs in the vocabulary. Many don't know what to pick up in the drug store, nor the dosages to take. The next topic is about dosage for medicines.
3. Drill verbs like *hurt, ache,* etc. The *question and answer drill* and *negative drill* is very important here. *Where do you hurt? Does your head hurt? No, my head doesn't hurt.* Insert other nouns like *throat, stomach,* etc. and continue the drill. You can get lots of sentences from students with these drills.
4. Demonstrate *It hurts here. Does it hurt here? No, not there. Here.* Demonstrate *up, down. It hurts up here, not down there.*

5. This topic brings out all the aches and pains and medical troubles. Be prepared to recommend a doctor. Realize that you are not medically trained, Say: *I'm not a doctor.* I use this. I call for help. I ask the pharmacist. *Do NOT practice medicine without a license.*
6. If they already know the above:
    a. Ask what other products they buy that are over-the-counter type. What illness do they use that product for?

Reading and Writing Exercises

1. Write model sentences on the board. *My father has pain in his stomach. It hurts him a lot. He hurts in his head too. He needs to see a doctor.* Have students read and copy the sentences.
2. Drill all the new verbs. Statement, question, negatives.

Competency

- I can ask for aspirin and cough drops.
- I can tell major parts of my body.
- I know pain, ache, sit down, etc.
- I can say where it hurts.

Materials You Will Need

- Boxes from the medicine cabinet. *Aspirin, antacids, cough drops, Pepto Bismal,* etc.
- Picture of the body for parts of the body.
- Simon says: Play *touch where it hurts.* (He's getting closer. Up a little, down, etc.)
- Have any handouts copied and ready for your class.

TOPIC SEVEN:
Body, Health, and Emergencies

VOCABULARY

Verbs

1. Hurt
2. Breathe in
3. Breathe out
4. Lie down
5. Get up
6. Stand up
7. Raise
8. Help
9. Throw up
10. Vomit
11. Burn
12. Dial
13. It hurts here!
14. Cough
15. Show me.

Prepositions

1. Up
2. Down

Opposites

1. Sick, Well
2. Good, Bad
3. Cheap, Expensive
4. Get up, Lie down

Nouns

1. Nurse
2. Doctor
3. Emergency
4. Throat
5. Stomach
6. Headache
7. Nosebleed
8. Medicine
9. Hospital
10. Ambulance
11. Call 911
12. Rash
13. Aspirin
14. Cough
15. Cough drop

Questions

1. How much does it hurt?
2. How much money does it cost?
3. What's wrong?

READING AND SPEAKING EXERCISE

Medical Situations

Where's Jose today

Where's Jose today?
He's home sick.
What's wrong?
He has a headache.

I need my medicine today.
Do I need my medicine?

Take a deep breath.
Breathe in, breathe out.

What can I buy for a _cough_?
What do you have for a headache?

My stomach aches.
My head aches.
I hurt all over.

Does it hurt?

Ouch! That hurts.

I'm in pain. It hurts very much.
Where does it hurt?
Does it hurt here?

I don't know.

It hurts up here.
Right here?
Right here?
Is this where it hurts?

Ouch! Ouch!.

Yes, It hurts there. Right down there.
Right here?
Right up here?

No, down. there.

My head hurts there.

Does Pedro need a doctor?

Does Pedro need a doctor?
No, a doctor is too expensive.

What can I do?
Make him lie down.
Make him sit up.

You have a rash.

What can I do to help?
Dial 911.

Point to your (mouth, etc.)
Touch your _______.
I need an aspirin.
You need a cough drop._____.

What do I take for it?

What do I take for my headache?

What do I take for it??
Take an aspirin.
Take an aspirin.
Go lie down and sleep.

What do I take for my cough?

What do I take for it?
Take a cough drop.
Drink lots of water and don't talk.

What do I take for my stomachache?

What do I take for it?
Take a tums.
Take an antacid pill.
It'll help.
It really will.

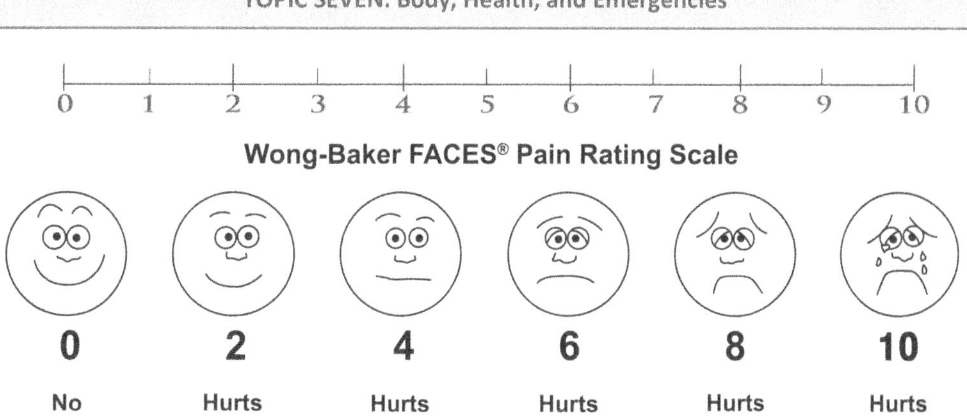

Instructions for Usage

Explain to the person that each face represents a person who has no pain (hurt), or some, or a lot of pain.

Face 0 doesn't hurt at all. Face 2 hurts just a little bit. Face 4 hurts a little bit more. Face 6 hurts even more. Face 8 hurt a whole lot. Face 10 hurts as much as you can imagine, although you don't have to be crying to have this worst pain.

Ask the person to choose the face that best depicts the pain they are experiencing

WRITING EXERCISE

Write the Sentences: *I feel good. Do you feel good today?*

I feel good. Do you feel good today?

Write the words: *It hurts, Breathe in, Stand up, It burns* in the spaces below.

It hurts			
Breathe in			
Stand up			
It burns			

Write the Sentences: *Is this an emergency? Yes, it is.* in the spaces below

Is this an emergency? Yes, it is.

Write the words: *Aspirin, Cough drops, Medicine, Rash, Hospital* in the spaces below.

Aspirin			
Cough drops			
Medicine			
Rash			
Hospital			

Write the words: *Nurse, Headache, Stomach, Call 911, Nosebleed* in the spaces below.

Nurse			
Headache			
Stomach			
Call 911			
Nosebleed			

Write the Sentences: *Where does it hurt? Right here.* in the spaces below

Where does it hurt? Right here.

Write the Sentence: *My mother is in the hospital.* in the spaces below

My mother is in the hospital.

Write the Question: *How much does it hurt?* in the spaces below

How much does it hurt?

Write the Question: *On a scale of 1 to 10, how much does it hurt?* in the spaces below

On a scale of 1 to 10, how much does it hurt?

Write the Sentence: *It's about a 6 today.* in the spaces below

It's about a 6 today.

Write the Sentence: *It really hurts a lot. It's about an 8.*

It really hurts a lot. It's about an 8.

TOPIC EIGHT TEACHER NOTES

Student Goals

- Identify measurements such as teaspoon, tablespoon, cup, etc.
- Say, *What is the dosage?*
- Know pill, capsule, tablet, drop, etc.
- Use *yesterday, today, tomorrow,* and *times to take medicine.* Example: Take two pills three times a day.

Notes to the teacher

The eighth topic should review health problems in parts of the body and understand the verbs to be used in medical situations. Help the students figure out dosages. Read the labels, if possible, on several bottles.

Suggestions

1. Once again, bring several items from your home medicine cabinet. Bring a cup, a teaspoon and a tablespoon. Show the items & demonstrate them.
2. TPR the dosage for medicines. Practice, drill and test the students hearing and understanding of the amounts. Make this a time the students have to talk and answer you.
3. Drill verbs. The question drill and the negative drill are very important here. How much do I swallow? Take one teaspoon.
4. This class brings out all the aches and pains and medical troubles. Be prepared to recommend a doctor. Realize that you are not medically trained, Say: I'm not a doctor. I use this. I call for help. I ask the pharmacist. Do NOT practice medicine without a license.
5. If there is a health packet, or a pharmacist willing to help, this is a good time to ask for help.
6. Teach meal times. Take one pill after each meal.
7. If they already know the above:
    a. Ask about other medicines they take. For example: high blood pressure.

Reading and Writing Exercises

1. Write model sentences on the board. Be sure students read with you, alone and with you again. Have them copy the Jazz Chant.

Materials You Will Need

- Measuring spoons to teach dosages of medicines: teaspoon (t), tablespoon (T), dropper, etc.
- Boxes from the medicine cabinet. Aspirin, antacids, cough drops, Pepto Bismal, etc.
- Picture of the body.
- Clock to teach mealtimes.
- Any handouts you will use, copied and ready for your class.

Competency

- I know *teaspoon*(t) and *tablespoon* (T) .
- I know *breakfast, lunch, & dinner.*
- I know *dosage* and whether it goes with or without meals.
- I know the meaning of, *swallow*.

TOPIC EIGHT:
Dosages for Medicines

VOCABLUARY

Verbs

1. Swallow
2. Drink
3. Measure
4. Taste
5. Must have
6. Take

Prepositions

1. During
2. After
3. With

Opposites

1. Sick, Well
2. Right, Wrong
3. Take, Give
4. With food, On empty stomach

Nouns

1. Pill
2. Food
3. Drugstore
4. Caplet, Pill
5. teaspoon (t)
6. Morning
7. Noon
8. Night
9. Lunch
10. Dinner
11. Tablespoon (T)
12. Glass
13. Drop
14. Pharmacist
15. Breakfast

Questions

1. How much do I take?
2. What's the right amount?

READING AND SPEAKING EXERCISE

When do I take my medicine?

When do I take my medicine?
When do I take it?

Take it every morning with a meal.

Take it every evening with a meal.

Don't forget. It's important.

When do I take my medicine?
When do I take it?

Take it every morning with a meal.

Take it every evening with a meal.

Don't forget. It's important.
Take this pill three times a day., morning, noon, and night.

Take it with water or milk?
Take it with water or milk?

Take it with food, and never on an empty stomach.

OK, I will.
OK. I will.

Three Times a day

How much do I take?
How much do I take?

One tablet three times a day.
One tablet three times a day.

One at breakfast, one at lunch, one with dinner. No more.

One at breakfast, one at lunch, one with dinner. No more.

How much should I give her?
How much should I give her?

One tablespoon every four hours. No more, no more.

One tablespoon every four hours. No more, no more.

Don't take it on an empty stomach. Be sure to eat.

Don't take it on an empty stomach. Be sure to eat.

Medicines and Dosages

1. How much do I give?

   Give the baby three drops twice a day.

   She cries.
   She must have the medicine.

2. He keeps coughing.
   He must take the cough syrup before he goes to sleep.

3. She's really sick.
   She feels bad.

4. What's the right amount to take?

   Take one pill three times a day.

   Take one tablespoon of cough medicine. Don't take it too often.

5. When do I take the medicine?

   Take it with meals.

   Do not take it on an empty stomach.

6. Do you have an aspirin?
   No, I only have a Tums.

WRITING EXERCISE

Write: *When do I take my medicine?* in all of the spaces below.

When do I take my medicine?

Write the words: *Take a pill, Once a day, With food, At dinner* in the spaces below.

Take a pill			
Once a day			
With food			
At dinner			

Write: *Can you swallow the pill?* in all of the spaces below.

Can you swallow the pill?

Write: *Yes, I can. I can swallow the pill.* in the spaces below.

Yes, I can. I can swallow the pill.

Write: ***No, I can't I can't swallow the pill.*** **in the spaces below.**

No, I can't. I can't swallow the pill.

Make the sentences below into a ***question*** **in the space that follows and a** ***negative*** **sentence in the next space. The first sentence is an example.**

Take this pill three times a day. (this is an example)
Do I take this pill three times a day?
I don't take this pill three times a day
Take this pill each evening.
I have a bottle of aspirin.

Write the words: *Measure, Taste, Swallow, With food, and Empty* in the spaces provided.

Taste			
Taste			
Swallow			
Swallow			
with Food			
with Food			
Empty			
Empty			

Write: *We eat dinner at 7:00 PM.* in all of the spaces below.

We eat dinner at 7:00 PM.

Write: ***What time do you eat breakfast?*** **in all of the spaces below.**

What time do you eat breakfast?

Write: ***I don't like this medicine.*** **in all of the spaces below.**

I don't like this medicine.

Write: ***Are you taking your medicine three times a day?*** **in all of the spaces below.**

Are you taking your medicine three times a day?

Copy the sentence that is on the left side into the space on the right side.

This is a sample.	This is a Sample.
I like it.	
I do not like it.	
I don't like it.	
Do you like it?	
I taste it.	
I do not taste it.	
I don't taste it.	
Do you taste it?	
I swallow it.	
I do not swallow it.	
I don't swallow it.	
Do you swallow it?	
I drink it.	
I do not drink it.	
I don't drink it.	
Do you drink it?	

Copy the sentence that is on the left side into the space on the right side.

This is a sample.	This is a Sample.
I measure it.	
I do not measure it.	
I don't measure it.	
Do you measure it?	
I have it.	
I do not have it.	
I don't have it.	
Do you have it?	
I hurt.	
I do not hurt.	
I don't hurt.	
Do you hurt?	
I breathe in.	
I do not breathe in.	
I don't breathe in.	
Do you breathe in?	

TOPIC NINE TEACHER NOTES

Goals for the Student

- Identify American money: major bills and coins.
- Make change correctly
- Ask for basic food items, and how much they cost
- Answer simple questions at the supermarket

Notes to the teacher

The ninth Topic should review or teach money, food names, and shopping terms.

Suggestions

1. Bring some money for the students to count and make change.
2. Teach the areas of the supermarket. Make big signs for Produce, Dairy, Seafood, Frozen Foods, Meats, etc. Place the signs around the class. Then have students place items in each section. (Milk and cheese in Dairy, Chicken in Meats, fruits and vegetables in produce.
3. Set up a checkout in the classroom. Role play or TPR going through the checkout. (Paper or plastic?).
4. Answer questions about grocery stores in your area. What foods do your students need?
5. Help them ask for the correct change when it is wrong.
6. If they already know the above:
    a. Ask about weights and measures (a pound of, a slice of, a tube of, a head of, a box of, a loaf of, etc.)

Reading and Writing exercises

1. Write model sentences on the board. Today I went shopping. I bought milk, bread, rice and beans. The chicken was expensive. The fruit was on sale.
2. Drill all the new verbs. Statement, question, negative.

Materials You Will Need

- Money to count. Include bills and coins.
- Some actual items from the food you have at home. Fruits, carrots, or whatever. Pictures of fruits and vegetable. A plastic bag and a paper bag.
- Signs for areas of a supermarket.
- Names & locations of supermarkets in your area.
- Any handouts you will use, copied and ready for your class.

Competency

- I know American money.
- I know aisles, plastic, paper.
- I can make change.
- I know 4 food words in English.

TOPIC NINE:
Money, Shopping, Food

VOCABULARY

Verbs

1. Buy, bought
2. Sell, sold
3. Have, had
4. Cost, cost
5. Broke, broken
6. Give, gave

Opposites

1. Right, left
2. Fresh, Frozen
3. Fresh, spoiled
4. Fresh, Canned

Nouns

1. Aisle
2. Dollar
3. Quarter
4. Dime
5. Nickel
6. Penny
7. Change
8. Plastic
9. Paper
10. Rice
11. Beans
12. Fruit
13. Meats
14. Chicken
15. Milk

Prepositions

1. Near

Questions

1. How much does it cost? I don't know.
2. How much money do you have? I'm broke.

READING AND SPEAKING EXERCISE

Where can I find the milk?

Excuse me, Where can I find the milk?

Where can I find the milk?
 In the back on the far right.
 In the back on the far right.
 It's near the meat counter.

Excuse me, where can I find the beans?

Where can I find the beans?
 On aisle six with the canned goods.
 On aisle six with the canned goods.

Do you have any canned tomatoes?
Do you have any taco shells?
 Sure we do.
 Look on aisle 4 for tomatoes and on aisle 3 for taco shells.

Thanks a lot.

Paper or Plastic?

Would you like paper or plastic?
 Oh, Plastic, I guess.

Paper or plastic?
 Plastic is fine.

Would you like to drive up?
 Yes, I think I would.

Would you like to drive up?
 Yes, I would.

What number is your cart?
What number is your cart?
 It's number nineteen.

Here's your change. $3.54
 Uh, oh. Would you count again, please?

Would you count again, please?
I gave you a twenty, not a ten.
 Oh, I'm sorry. Here's your ten.
 Your change is $13.54.
 I'm so sorry.
That's OK. Have a nice day.

It's spoiled

I don't like that.
It tastes spoiled.

Bill, can I borrow a dollar.
I'll pay you back on Friday.
 Sorry, friend. I'm broke.

It Costs too much

It costs too much, doesn't it.
 Yes. I wish I had the money.

Do you want paper or plastic?
 Paper, please.
OK.

WRITING EXERCISE

Write the Sentences: ***I bought rice yesterday. I cook rice every day.*** **in the spaces below**

I bought rice yesterday. I cook rice every day.

Write the words: ***Quarter, Dime, Nickel, Penny***

Quarter				
Dime				
Nickel				
Penny				

Write the Sentence: ***Can you pick me up at 10?***

Can you pick me up at 10?

Write the Sentence: ***No, I can't.***

No, I can't.

Write the Sentence: ***The rice is near the beans on aisle 3.***

The rice is near the beans on aisle 3.

Write the Sentence: ***Can I borrow ten dollars until Friday?***

Can I borrow ten dollars until Friday?

Write the Sentence: ***I don't have change for $20.***

I don't have change for $20.

Write the words: ***Milk, Chicken, Rice, Beans, Fruit.***

Milk				
Chicken				
Rice				
Beans				
Fruit				

Write the Sentence: ***The meat I bought yesterday is spoiled.***

The meat I bought yesterday is spoiled.

Write the Sentence: ***I want some fresh fruit, not canned fruit.***

I want some fresh fruit, not canned fruit.

Write the Sentence: ***One quarter is 25 cents.***

One quarter is 25 cents.

Write the Sentence: ***Four quarters make one dollar.***

Four quarters make one dollar.

(Example) Write the *negative, negative with a contraction*, and as a *question* for the sentence in the first row.

Sentence:	I buy rice.
Negative::	**I do not buy rice.**
Negative contraction	**I don't buy rice.**
Question:	**Do I buy rice?**

(Example) Write the *negative, negative with a contraction*, and as a *question* for the sentence in the first row.

Sentence:	I bought rice yesterday.
Negative::	**I did not buy rice yesterday.**
Negative contraction	**I didn't buy rice yesterday.**
Question:	**Did I buy rice yesterday?**

Write the *negative, negative with a contraction*, and as a *question* for the sentence in the first row.

Sentence:	I have beans.
Negative::	
Negative contraction	
Question:	

Write the *negative, negative with a contraction*, and as a *question* for the sentence in the first row.

Sentence:	I had beans.
Negative::	
Negative contraction	
Question:	

Write the *negative, negative with a contraction*, and as a *question* for the sentence in the first row.

Sentence:	It cost too much.
Negative::	
Negative contraction	
Question:	

Write the *negative, negative with a contraction*, and as a *question* for the sentence in the first row.

Sentence:	I broke the dish.
Negative::	
Negative contraction	
Question:	

Write the *negative, negative with a contraction*, and as a *question* for the sentence in the first row.

Sentence:	You give money every week.
Negative::	
Negative contraction	
Question:	

Write the *negative, negative with a contraction*, and as a *question* for the sentence in the first row.

Sentence:	He gave money last week.
Negative::	
Negative contraction	
Question:	

TOPIC TEN TEACHER NOTES

Goals for the Student

- Order two simple items at a fast food restaurant.
- Know small, medium, and large
- Ask for ketchup or salt.
- Answer the, "Here or to go?" question.

Notes to the teacher

The tenth topic should discuss & teach fast food restaurants. The drive in window is not encouraged because the intercoms are so difficult to use and to understand, even for native speakers. Try to go to a fast food place before you teach this topic.

Suggestions

1. Bring some napkins, trays, etc. to class.
2. Role play buying food. Make change. Use the dialogs above and explain what is being asked.
3. Answer questions about fast food restaurants in your area. What foods do your students like to order. Ask them about it.
4. Help them ask for the correct change when it is wrong. Help them use a coupon.
5. If they already know the above:
    a. Change the orders to make special or large complicated things. Ask about several different kinds of fast food restaurants. Talk about cafeterias.

Reading and Writing Exercises

1. Write model restaurant menu of the board. Talk about the items that are offered. Bring in menus from pizza restaurants, etc.
2. Drill all the shorthand ways of ordering that you can think of. Write the "translations" on the board and have them copy them.

Competency

- I know the general layout of a fast food place.
- I know here or to go.
- I can ask for ketchup or a straw.
- I can order two items.

Materials You Will Need

- Ketchup and salt packets, napkins, and perhaps menus from fast food places.
- Some items that can be used in the role play, like a coke paper cup and a straw. Think out the role play and have as many items handy as possible.
- Set up some kind of counter and eating area. Make the classroom a "restaurant."
- Map of the restaurant, locating restrooms, condiment areas, etc.
- Think about McDonald's and a Sub shop. How do they differ?
- Take cell phone or tablet pictures of the menu you find in several familiar fast food restaurants in your area. Use them in class to help the students learn the vocabulary. These restaurants can be regional ones.

TOPIC TEN:
Fast Food Restaurants

VOCABULARY

Verbs present & past tense	Adverbs
1. Take, took	1. Over there
2. Pay, paid	2. Over here

Phrases

1. Who's next?	4. I have a coupon.
2. Here or to go?	5. May I take your order?
3. Everything all right?	6. Sweet or unsweetened?

Nouns

1. Hamburger	6. Napkins	11. Coupon
2. French fries	7. Fork	12. Cookie
3. Coke	8. Ketchup	13. Biscuit
4. Iced tea	9. Salt	14. Chicken
5. Tray	10. Order	15. Salad

Question words	Examples
1. How	How do you use a straw?
2. How	This is how you use a straw.

COMPETENCY

- I know the general layout of a fast food place.
- I know *here* or *to go.*
- I can ask for *ketchup* or a *straw*.
- I can order two items.

READING AND SPEAKING EXERCISE

Who's next?

Who's next?
Oh, I am.

What would you like?
I'd like two cokes.

What size, medium or large?
Large.

Burger and Fries

May I take your order?
Hamburger and fries.

Here or to go?
To go, please.

Everything all right?
I need some ketchup.

May I Take Your Order?

May I take your order?
Yes. I'd like two hamburgers, a french fry and a coke.
Oops. I mean two cokes.

Here or to go?
I'm eating here.

Here you go. Anything else?
I'd like ketchup.

It's on your tray.

It's four fifty.
Oh, I have a coupon.

Good. That'll save you a dollar. Three-fifty.

Thanks.

I'd Like a Sub Sandwich

What would you like today?
I'd like a sub sandwich.
I'd like a ham and cheese.

Wheat or white?
Wheat or white?
Wheat bread.

Everything on it?
No onion or pepper.

Thanks.

Anything to drink?
Cuppa coffee.

Anything in it?
With sugar and cream.
With sugar and cream.

OK. Comin' up.

Write the Sentence: ***Small hamburger, fries and a Coke, please.***

Small hamburger, fries and a Coke, please.

Write the words: ***Napkin, Fork, Ketchup, Catsup, Salt.***

Napkin				
Fork				
Ketchup				
Catsup				
Salt				

Write the Sentence: ***I'd like ketchup.*** **in the spaces below**

I'd like ketchup.

Write the Sentence: *I'd like catsup.* in the spaces below. (Note: catsup is an alternate spelling for ketchup.)

I'd like catsup.

Write the Sentence: *Where are the straws?*

Where are the straws?

Write the Sentence: *Where is the restroom?*

Where is the restroom?

Copy the sentences into the blank lines that follow.

I have a coupon.
Unsweetened tea, please.
I'd like to order a cup of coffee.

Write the words: *Medium, Small, Large, Hot, Sweet* in the spaces below.

Medium				
Small				
Large				
Hot				
Sweet				

Write the Sentence: ***I'd like a sub on wheat bread.***

I'd like a sub on wheat bread.

Write the Sentence: ***I want chicken salad.***

I want chicken salad.

Write the Sentence: ***I want that with fries.***

I want that with fries.

Write the *negative, negative with a contraction*, and as a *question* for the sentence in the first row.

Sentence:	I order.
Negative::	
Negative contraction	
Question:	

Write the *negative, negative with a contraction*, and as a *question* for the sentence in the first row.

Sentence:	I pay now.
Negative::	
Negative contraction	
Question:	

Write the *negative, negative with a contraction*, and as a *question* for the sentence in the first row.

Sentence:	I take.
Negative::	
Negative contraction	
Question:	

TOPIC ELEVEN TEACHER NOTES

Goals for the Student

- Ask for stamps. Know how to buy stamps.
- Know how to purchase a money order.
- Know *Pay To* and *Purchaser*.
- Address an envelope correctly.

Notes to the teacher

The eleventh topic should discuss the post office and sending a money order to their home country. Many students work to be able to send the money home. If you have never bought a money order, try to do it. The experience will help.

Suggestions

1. Bring some stamps and envelopes to class. You can recycle old envelops from your junk mail for students to practice on.
2. Role-play buying stamps. Make change. Ask for a receipt.
3. Answer questions about mail in your area. Go to the post office and find out what you don't know.
4. Ask a student you know if you can go to the post office with him or her.

Materials You Will Need

- Stamps and envelopes. Old envelopes to practice addressing.
- Sample money order. Perhaps the real thing.
- Set up Post Office role-play situations.
- Some change to count.

Reading and Writing Exercises

- Fill out a sample money order together.
- Work on weights and measurements.

Skills to practice:

- Writing on the lines in small print.
- Counting change.
- Asking for assistance.
- Pointing out incorrect change.

Concepts to teach

- The uses of the money order.
- Holding onto one's receipt.
- Gray area on the form
- Use a Ball Point Pen. Black or blue ink.
- Have some kind of positive identification, when and if necessary.

Teaching Technique

1. Present a situation where money must be sent through the mail. Include needing the receipt that you paid the money. Examples: There is a money emergency at home. You must pay a bill or a fee. You must pay money back to your brother.
2. Use flash cards to introduce vocabulary.
3. Practice with a listening exercise. Say the words quickly, and then have the students say them, so they will recognize them when a clerk speaks.
4. If they already know the above:
    a. Talk about other writing problems. Have an exercise with listening for the correct numbers and amounts.

Competency

- I know how to ask for stamps.
- I can get change.
- I can ask for a money order.
- I can keep the receipt.

TOPIC ELEVEN: Post Office and Money Orders

VOCABULARY

Verbs

1. Write, To write
2. Address, To address
3. Spell, To spell
4. Copy, To copy
5. Repeat, To repeat
6. Send, To send
7. Pay for, To pay for
8. Mail, To mail

Phrases

1. Who's next?
2. Where's it going?
3. That'll be seven fifty.
4. I need to buy ....
5. How much will it cost?
6. What's inside?
7. What are the contents?

Nouns

1. Copy
2. Money order
3. Receipt
4. Stamps
5. Change
6. Pay To
7. Amount
8. Envelope
9. Letter
10. Package
11. Contents
12. Purchaser
13. Stub
14. First class
15. Return address
16. Third class
17. Airmail
18. Postal Clerk

READING AND SPEAKING EXERCISE

Who's next?
  Oh, I am.
  I'd like a money order.

For how much?
  Seventy-five dollars.

Where's it going?
  Mexico city.

That'll be Seventy-eight dollars, please.

Anything else?
  I need a receipt.

The blue copy is your receipt. Keep the stub from the money order.
  Thanks.
I need a post office box.
How much will one cost?
  $2.00 a month.

Going to Mexico?
OK. What's inside the package?
  Some clothes, and drugstore items, like aspirin and antihistamines.
OK. That'll be 8.75.

Anything else?
  I need a money order for 50 dollars.

Sure.
  How long will it take.

A coupla weeks. Not so long for third class.
  For first class?
Be there the end of the week.
  How much does each cost?
First class costs ----.
Third class costs ---.
  I'll take third class. Thanks.

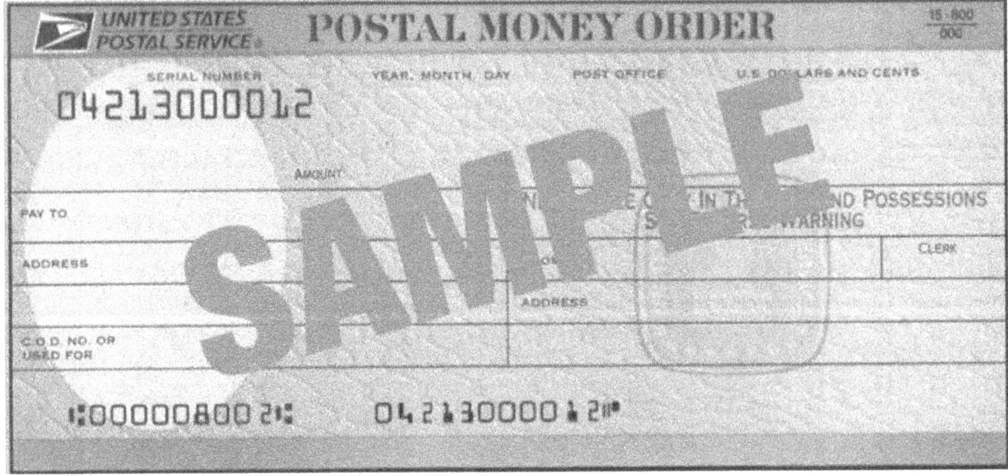

Who's Next?

Who's next?
What can I do for you?
  I need some stamps.
  I need to send these letters.

Sure. Where're they going?
  To Mexico.
  To my hometown,....

That'll be fifty cents a letter.
Fifty cents each.
  OK. Three letters.
  Three stamps.
  One-fifty.

That's right.
  Thanks.

Write Home, Please.

Write home, Pedro.
Write home, please.
  What'll I say?
  So much work, so little pay.

Write home, Pedro.
Write home anyway.
  What'll I say?
  English is hard.
  Everything costs a lot.

Say that. Tell your mom.
Tell your mom we're OK.
  I don't have stamps.
  I don't have money to send her.
  I'm too tired to write.

I'll go to the post office with you.
  OK. I'll write.
  We'll go together.

Write the Sentence: *I'd like to buy a money order.*

I'd like to buy a money order.

Write the words: *Receipt, Stamps, Change, Envelop*

Receipt				
Stamps				
Change				
Envelop				

Write the Sentence: *Keep your receipt and stub.*

Keep your receipt and stub.

Write the question: *How long will it take to arrive?*

How long will it take to arrive?

Write the question: *What are the contents of the package?*

What are the contents of the package?

Copy the sentences into the blank lines that follow.

I need ten stamps.
Do you have change for a dollar?
I'll send it first class.

Write the words: *Write, Spell, Address, Copy, Send* in the spaces below.

Write				
Spell				
Address				
Copy				
Send				

Copy the sentences into the blank lines that follow.

How do you spell your name?
I need a copy.
I'll send it second class.

Copy the sentences into the blank lines that follow.

Can you spell?	No, I can't spell.
I think you can spell.	Yes I can spell.
Can you send it to mom?	No, I can't send it to mom.
I think you can.	Yes, I can send it.
Can you pay for it?	No, I can't pay for it.
You have to pay for it.	Yes, I can pay for it.

How to buy a USA postal money order:

1. Have the amount in cash plus the fee for each money order you want to buy. You will have to pay a small fee for the money order.
2. Go to the U.S. Post Office.
3. Wait in line to see a postal clerk.
4. Tell the postal clerk: "I need a money order for___ dollars, please."
5. Pay the cash for the money order. Remember there is an extra fee charge.
6. Count your change.
7. Fill out the money order with the *Pay To* name and address, and the *Purchaser* name and address.
8. Keep the customer receipt or stub.
9. Send the money order.

TOPIC TWELVE TEACHER NOTES

Goals for the student

- Locate major streets on a map.
- Know names of public buildings.
- Be able to give directions from one area to another.
- Be able to give directions inside a building from one area to another.
- Ask directions to a place, for example: Where can I find the gas station?

Notes to the teacher

The twelfth topic should discuss the community, giving directions, and reading a local map. Mark several places on the map before you start.

Suggestions

1. Bring maps of your area to class. You can draw a pretend map on the board.
2. Role play directions. Mark certain areas in the classroom and move chairs to make roads and blocks. Have one student give directions in the classroom or teaching area, and another student follows them.
3. Answer questions about locations of things in your area.
4. Teach north, south, east, and west.
5. Teach how to say letters, like GPS.
6. Obtain a map of your state. Have the students plan a trip to another part of the state. Have them orally explain their trip to the class.

7. Assign the students to make a travel poster of a place to visit in your area.
8. Trace bus or train routes on your county or city map.
9. If they already know most of the lesson, go deeper:
    a. Talk about other location and driving problems. Talk about road signs and driver's license.

Reading and Writing Exercises

1. Write a model paragraph. Fit the streets and directions to your area.

Wells Fargo Bank is in Falls Village Shopping Center. From the beltline, I-440, go north 2.75 miles. You'll go through many red lights. You'll pass main roads like Millbrook Road and Spring Forest Road. Falls Village is located on the corner of Sandy Forks Road and Falls of the Neuse Road. You'll see a large Exxon station on the corner. It's across from the country club. Wells Fargo Bank is next to the Exxon Station.

Competency

- I can ask for directions.
- I can count blocks and red lights.
- I know turn left, right.
- I can say three letters (like GPS, or CBS, etc.) correctly.
- I can read major roads on a map.

Materials You Will Need

- Maps of your area. Perhaps a state highway map.
- Direction signs. North, south, east, west.
- Street signs and building signs to role play directions.
- Masking tape or chalk to draw streets on the classroom floor.
- Something to represent a traffic light, and a stop sign

TOPIC TWELVE:
Maps and the Community

VOCABULARY

Verbs

1. To turn (around)
2. To walk
3. To identify
4. To know
5. To drive
6. To search (for)
7. To repeat
8. To draw
9. To travel

Phrases

1. Where's the ____? (school)
2. Go straight ahead.
3. Turn left., Turn right.
4. Go about a mile.
5. Keep going.
6. Count the traffic lights.
7. Which way?
8. Turn around.
9. Go around the block.
10. Go around the corner.

Nouns

1. Block
2. Corner
3. Right
4. Left
5. Straight ahead
6. GPS
7. Bank
8. Stop sign
9. Red light.
10. Library
11. Laundromat
12. Gas station
13. Hospital
14. School
15. Office building

Directions

1. North
2. South
3. East
4. West

READING AND SPEAKING EXERCISE

The laundromat

Where's the laundromat?

About a mile down Main Street. It's across from the gas station.

Could you repeat that please?

The gas station

I need some gas. Where's the gas station?

Go three red lights. It's around the corner.

Thanks. That's three red lights and around the corner?

Sure. That's right.

I'm lost

I'm lost. Can you help me find the church?

Yes. Go straight ahead. Turn on Main Street. It's next to McDonald's.

Which way?

Which way to I-95?

Go north about a mile on this road. Then turn left. It's straight ahead about 5 miles.

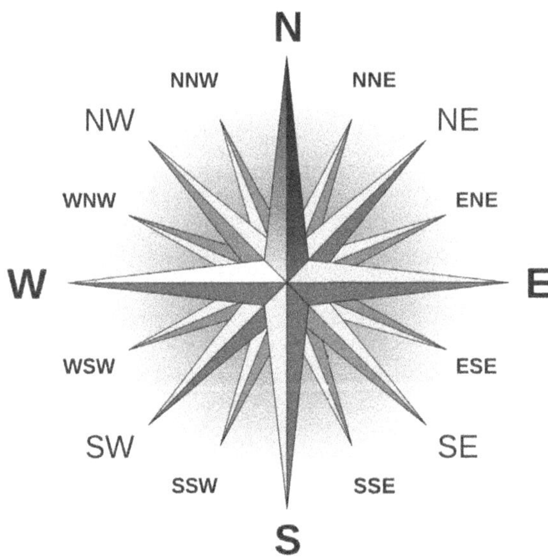

Directions

He talks too fast. What'll I do?
He talks too fast. Where'll I go?
I'll ask someone new.

> The bank? Oh, it's on Six Forks Road.
> Turn right at the next light.
> Then go straight for two miles.
> It's on the corner of Six Forks and Millbrook.

Say it again, please.
Repeat it, please.

> It's on Six Forks Road.
> Turn right at the next light.
> Then go straight for two miles.
> It's on the corner of Six Forks and Millbrook.

Thanks, Mister.
I think I can find it now.
It's on Six Forks road.
Turn right at the next light.
Then go straight for two miles.
It's on the corner of Six Forks and Millbrook.
Thanks a lot.

> No problem.

Count the red lights.

Where is it?
Where is it?
I though you knew.
I thought you knew.

> I did too. Now I'm lost.
> What did he say?
> What did he say?

He said, "count the red lights."
He said, "count the red lights."

> I'll go back. We'll try again.
> I'll go back. We'll try again.
> I'll turn around. We'll count together.
> I'll turn around. We'll count together.

Did he say three lights?
Did he say three lights?

> I think so.
> Yes, he did.

OK. That's one, two, three.

> Whew! That's it. On the corner.
> Whew! That's it. On the corner.

"Letter Words"

Do not try to say these as words. Instead, pronounce the letters individually. For example, with GPS, you say "G-P-S", not "geeps"

1. GPS	4. IBM	7. RSVP	10. ESL
2. CBS	5. NBC	8. IRS	11. USCIS
3. AT&T	6. ABC	9. FBI	12. USA

WRITING EXERCISE

Write the Sentences: *I need a map of this state.*

I need a map of this state.

Write the words: *Traffic, Block, Repeat, Identify*

Traffic				
Block				
Repeat				
Identify				

Write the Sentences: ***Count the traffic signals.***

Count the traffic signals.

Write the Sentences: ***Make a U-turn.***

Make a U-turn.

Write the Sentence: ***Turn around at the next street.***

Turn around at the next street.

Copy the sentences into the blank lines that follow.

I think I can find it now.
Turn right and then go straight ahead.
Where is the nearest hospital?

Write the words: *Gas, Station, GPS, Copy, Send* in the spaces below.

Gas				
Station				
GPS				
Copy				
Send				

Copy the sentences into the blank lines that follow.

I have a GPS. I can find your house.
Say it again, please

Copy the sentences into the blank lines that follow.

Can I drive?	No, I can't drive.
I think you can drive.	Yes, I can drive.
Do you have a GPS?	No, I don't have a GPS.
I think you do.	Yes, I have a GPS.
Can you understand it?	No, I can't understand it.
I think you can.	Yes, I can understand it.

ABOUT THE AUTHOR

Glenda Reece has been a teacher, a trainer, an author, and a content creator for ESL and Cross Culture programs from Alaska to Florida; and has trained foreign speaking ESL teachers in China and South America. Her work has ranged from the North Carolina Governor's committee for refugee resettlement to high school ESL teacher to business owner to Literacy volunteer.

She has taught or led seminars for the Immigration and Refugee Center, the National Association of Foreign Student Advisors (NAFSA), Teachers of English to Speakers of Other Languages (TESOL), Southeastern Seminary, North Carolina State University, the University of North Carolina, Duke University, Wake County School System, and at Literacy Conferences for Baptist State Conventions in numerous states.

Glenda is the owner of ESL Training Service, which provides English and Cross Cultural training to international business professionals in the Raleigh, NC, area. She was an early president of the North and South Carolina chapter of TESOL. She has been recognized by the Baptist State Convention of North Carolina as Literacy Volunteer of the Year, and was presented the Mildred Blankenship National Volunteer of the Year Award by the North American Mission Board of the Southern Baptist Convention.

She is the author of a two-volume ESL textbook, *English Lessons from the Bible: The Book of Mark*. Student and Teacher versions of these books, which have been in continuous publication since 1989, are available at Lifeway.com. They are sold at cost and without royalties to the author. The books have been used in programs, both Christian and secular, in every corner of the globe.

Glenda has produced several training videos including *Conversational English Using the Lipson Method*, *The Oral Interview Procedure,* and *Getting Serious About Top-Down and Bottom-Up Pronunciation.*